SISTERHOOD

JULIE R. ENSZER

Julie R Enszer

Debbie —
Celebrate
Sisterhood!
Julie
December 2013

SIBLING RIVALRY PRESS
ALEXANDER, ARKANSAS
WWW.SIBLINGRIVALRYPRESS.COM

Sisterhood

Sibling Rivalry Press, LLC
13913 Magnolia Glen Drive
Alexander, AR 72002

info@siblingrivalrypress.com

www.siblingrivalrypress.com

ISBN: 978-1-937420-57-4

Library of Congress Control Number: 20139450221

First Sibling Rivalry Press Edition, November 2013

For Lara, always absent, and Kim, forever present.

A TABLE OF PARTS:

TITLES AND PAGE NUMBERS

SISTERHOOD

All I really want is some comfort
A way to get my hands untied
And all I really want is some justice. . . .

—ALANIS MORISSETTE

Time after
Sometimes you picture me
I'm walking too far ahead.

—CYNDI LAUPER

I.

MOON

At forty, my menses
settle on twenty-eight
days, unmoved by my
wife's cycle, unaffected
by time with other
women. I always bleed on
Passover, Sukkot, Purim.
My blood, bathed in light.
My body, regular, certain,
pulled not by my sisters
but by the lunar cycle.
The moon and I wax
and wane synchronously.
At menarche, my mother
told me about the curse,
welcomed me to a tribe
of bitterness, unhappiness,
lost ambitions. She said
I would never get what
I wanted. I could feel
dreams seeping out
between my legs, wiped
away with cheap cotton,
flushed into a river
of despair. She told me
one day this curse
would be a gift:
I would make babies.
From feminists, I learned
the mystical power
of menstrual blood—
womantime, wombtime—
how nuns and lesbians
in land communities

menstruated together,
sloughing off life
unfulfilled. I want to live
among the devout.
Our periodic blood
a sign of piety, communal
autonomy. My menses never
conjured magic. My body
never bore children.
The most mystical I
become is the moment
before Seder, tired
from cooking, cleaning,
I sit on the lanai, hungry,
crampy. I imagine
the moon. Sister-witness.
Long after I stop
bleeding, the moon will rise.
This is my burden.
This, my joy.

MY DNA

Vibrating a femtosecond here,
a millisecond there, the base
pairs are always moving.
Holes opening and closing

through the center;
electrons migrating.
It is like a cocktail party:
nothing stays still.

Every minute of our life,
even after death, our DNA
squirms and sparks.
So twitchy, so reliable.

If it had been up to me,
I would have gambled
with Pauling and Corey:
our DNA, a triple helix,

a tripartite life force written
deep inside. I'd have given
the winning double
to Watson and Crick.

Yet, even with its frenzied
energy, zipping, swelling,
teeming with life, I wonder: is our
double helix sometimes lonely?

Lonely like me? Like my
one living sister?
Does it secretly wish
it was a triple helix?

HAMSTER

> *It is the responsibility of the poet to be a woman   to keep an eye on*
> *this world and cry out like Cassandra, but be*
> *listened to this time.*
> —Grace Paley, "Responsibility"

When I was six or seven
my sisters and I had one.
We kept it in our room,
changed its cage,
but approached it with fear.
It was more my father's pet.
I think he hoped
our fascination and repulsion
would translate someday
to scientific research—we might
trade hamsters for rats or rabbits,
a quest to discover cancer cures,
find keys to genetic mysteries—
but none of us would hold it
in our hands as father did,
let it run up and down our arms,
around our neck. We held it
by the vestigial tail, and,
when it squirmed too much,
we'd scream, drop it on the bed.
The first time, flustered,
we trapped it with a bowl,
then worried how it would breath.
We fashioned a shoebox with holes
for weekly cage cleaning.
That summer, returning home
from a week-long vacation,
we found it dead. No food.
No water. I don't remember
who was supposed to plan

for hamster's basic needs.
We wrapped it in a matchbox
shrouded with paper towels,
buried it in our back yard. It was
the first time I saw my father cry.
At night, I missed the hamster's
scurry amidst shredded newspaper,
the squeak of its exercise wheel,
the faint glug of the water dispenser.
It was the first time I realized
what happens if I don't fulfill
my responsibilities.
Since then, I've failed many things.
Physics in college and
organic chemistry. The Women's
Crisis Center—closed because
I didn't raise enough money.
A master's degree in Social Work—
I paid the tuition but left
one paper unwritten.
Many friends now dead from AIDS.
The city of Detroit—burgeoning
on a renaissance, needing
young residents. I moved away.
My sister. I meant to call her
the night before the fatal car accident.
The abolition of nuclear weapons.
Liberation for gays and lesbians.
Reducing CO_2 emissions.
These all, my responsibilities.
Until today. Today, I put
responsibility in a shoe box
swaddled with a well-worn shirt
and your obituary, Grace.
Bury it beneath the old oak
that each spring flings acorns
loudly on our tile roof. Each
click and clack and bong

remind me of new responsibilities:
my mind, this one body,
these words. Listen.

THE FORMER PRIME MINISTER

I hate how these women hide themselves
beneath head scarves; for once I don't disagree,
I sip my Diet Coke; I look at the woman
two tables away, a few strands
of hair have fallen across her face;
I want to tuck them in.
In twelve hours, I will be at the airport,
stamped and ready to leave for Thailand;
I will be exhausted and sick. It is ironic:
a sore throat, not from my talking
but from silence in the face of
the rhetoric of the former prime minister—
he wants to incite opposition
to the U.S. war, so he throws
verbal red meat to the largely
Muslim crowd. The Jews this;
the Jews that. *The Jooosss control America;*
the Jooosss control the banks;
the Jooosss control Hollywood.
Unoriginal. Misguided. Wrong.
But I tell myself, there is no Muslim
leader who doesn't serve up
such pork fat to his people.
I am uncomfortable but silent;
I get a massage,
I buy a Turkoman carpet.
The next afternoon he speaks
in solidarity with the holocaust denier
jailed in Austria, he asks,
Where is his freedom of speech?
Ironic from one who jailed many:
children from Australia,
his own deputy P.M. He asks,
Why can we not question the number six million?

He asks, *What if it was 5,999,999?*
He passes this off as a joke.
Then, he talks about Auschwitz.
He says, *There was nothing*
found there after the war. No camp. No oven.
That evening, my travel companion and I
boycott the final formal dinner;
I stare at the hair of the woman
two tables over. Early the next morning,
shrouded by darkness,
I will go to the airport.
I will think about Zarina,
the woman wearing a Donatella Versace
scarf as a hajib; pink, grey, and textured,
made from the finest silk.
I will wonder if she bought it in Italy.
I will wonder if she spoke to the shop clerk
in her perfect, British-accented English
or if she spoke perfect Italian, also with a British accent.
I want to touch her scarf, her head, her hair.
I study the lines beneath her scarf:
her ears, her tied up hair, her skull.
I imagine them as my own.
I want to believe in some sort of transcendent,
feminist sisterhood: Donatella, Zarina, and me.
I want to believe Zarina isn't thinking
about the final solution for the Jews.
My throat hurts. I tie my hair back in a knot.
I board the plane. I walk away.

MY MOTHER'S VANITY

Visiting, I need to wash my hands.
She replaced the vanity with this *au courant*
oak cabinet when Ronald Reagan was
President. There is only a small space

for water to drizzle into the faux marble sink;
the bathroom is packed. Pots and palettes,
powders, compacts, and applicators
stored ramshackle in plastic containers.

I want a trash bag to empty it all:
counter, small shelf, back of the toilet,
the entire medicine chest. I want to throw
it all away. Give my mother a clean

slate, but I wash my hands. Rub soap
from a pile of four half-used bars
then dry on threadbare hand towels
and walk downstairs. There are no new

beginnings, no fresh starts for mother,
only a lifetime collection of make-up—
mauve, purple, burgundy, silver.
The many reasons my face is bare.

MY FATHER'S PORNOGRAPHY

One hot July day when I was thirteen
my best friend and I snatched the mail
from the carrier as he inserted it
through the slot in the front door.
No penpal letters, no catalogues,
no real correspondence, but carte blanche
from my father to open his junk mail.
I tore into the thick, black, plastic package
and found glossy paper with small
squares of color popping up from the dark
background. Inside, pictures. Things
I'd never imagined. Men with penises
in their mouths, men showing their asses,
men with what I would later learn to call
long, hard cocks and hairy balls.
For the first time, I saw outside the triangle
of my house, my friend, and the local 7-11
into a world where people didn't marry
college sweethearts, return to hometowns,
and teach at their alma mater. A world
where people watched something
besides television, lived without children,
ate at restaurants with waiters,
bought gourmet groceries,
traveled to places without shopping malls,
and wore watches that didn't say Timex.
There, desire was telegraphed in public
with tattoos, silver, and Levis, and sex
happened outside cotton-poly sheets.
It was the world I wanted to enter.
Holding those pictures, I knew
I would not stay in Saginaw
for the same reasons, twenty-five

years later, my father could not escape.
Then, my horrified mother yanked the photos
from my fascinated hands, cursing me
and my very best friend and my father,
and we never spoke of this again.

ZYKLON B

Where should one draw the line?
. . . the line is very clearly Zyklon B.

The painters call before we move into the new house.
Ma'am, they say—
I am not old enough to be a ma'am, but I don't correct
them—
Ma'am, they say, *we smell gas.*
I dismiss their concern. I say, *Keep painting.*
I say, *You are already two weeks behind schedule.*

Five days after we move in, I wake up sick. I vomit.
Gas filled our house. We open all the windows,
call the utility company. The stove regulator isn't working.
It can't be fixed. We buy a new Frigidaire.

This is what I know of life:
Love fiercely, even recklessly;
Laugh loudly, even raucously;
Risk everything, at least once;
Live openly, without abandon;
Build trust, be honest;
Buy American.

A year later our washing machine breaks.
I want a new German one—small, sleek, stylish.
I tell my wife, *It is perfect for the kitchen.*
Our washer and dryer are in the kitchen.
My wife says, *They built the ovens.*
We buy a new Frigidaire.

Degesch, a company affiliated with Degussa,
based in Dusseldorf,
is the world's largest maker of specialty chemicals.
Degussa has an exemplary record

of examining the wartime past,
making restitution to victims. Still
The Memorial Foundation for the Murdered Jews of Europe
rejects a subcontract for Degussa.
Degesch manufactured gas pellets: Zyklon B.

This is what I know of gas:
May you never make a mistake that cannot be corrected.
May you never take an action that cannot be forgotten.

RESISTING SIBILANCE

The curse of the firstborn
is the persistent document
of our young lives. Baby
pictures, scraps of hair,

foot prints, hand prints,
all stored in perpetuity.
My father kept a record
of every word I spoke

before the age of one.
I don't remember them
(or actually I do
remember—the words,

that is, still having
linguistic use for terms
such as ball, cat, and
Dada). What I don't

recall are the infant
vocalizations, the initial
aspirations of sound against
my new teeth, my young lips.

My sister, the youngest,
resisted language much longer
with two older sibs
to satisfy. We responded

incessantly to her physical
movements, pointing
and grabbing, her
guttural evocations.

Soon she was six, speech
impaired, seeing a
therapist until her language
repaired. Still she will

always be to me
resisting sibilance,
crooning childlike:
lippery eal, lippery eal.

MY NAME IS ETHYL

My father wanted to name
his daughters Ethyl, Methyl, and Propyl;
I would have been Ethyl, the eldest.
Perhaps that explains my affinity
for another Ethel—Rosenberg—
who I saw again this weekend
at the refurbished American Art Museum.
First, a photograph of her with Julius
in a paddy wagon during their trials—
it's trying to remember the pain
of Ethel, so young and so beautiful
in that hard-working way of socialist women.
Then, a sketch in the portrait gallery:
Ethel's disembodied head—no neck—
adapted from a snapshot for a protest
poster; the artist captured
her jaw set with purpose,
her clear eyes so certainly innocent,
her frizzy hair, a utilitarian halo
around her determined head, oh, yes,
Ethel . . . but my father would not
have named me for you, Ethel, rather
for those basic organic molecules—
all grown, you are as basic to me
as ethyl to a student of chemistry.
Although when I was younger,
I wanted to be my sister, heir to the name
Propyl. I imagined us calling
her Iso for short and my other sister Di,
but the joke would have been
only in our family—it would never
have translated to the hard-scrabble
streets of Saginaw. For that reason
and many others, my mother resisted

my father's chemical compounds;
we have bland names, we blend in,
until you meet us, until we speak.
Then you can imagine Ethel,
her grey coat, sturdy shoes, curly hair,
that look of defiance in our eyes.

TIME PIECE

Do you remember hospital visits?
Medicine too toxic to be touched
by human hands and dispensed
throughout the day? Do you remember
digital watches with multiple alarms?
One friend wore two on each wrist,
all of different colors. They beeped
asynchronously; this one for pills
with milk; this for pills on an empty
stomach; these two with meals.
We marveled at the small
slender chips precisely tracking
time. We raged at the disease,
at the way treatment was worse
than the ailment and offered no cure,
at how no one cared about the burden
of so many time pieces shackling
one's wrist. In the end, wasting,
the watches drooped to his palms.
We poked more holes
into their plastic bands.
We believed in the magic of time,
in the possibility of small pills.
Keep on the regimen, we whispered,
New drugs in the pipeline.
We crooned reassurances,
crossed our fingers and toes
when he sat on the toilet.
On good days, the door open
for a stream of new magazines
and hushed conversation;
on bad days, closed. Nothing
but silence. In the end,

it didn't matter—digital alarms,
the precise measurement of time.
His ran out.

BROKEN-HEARTED

Alone for the first time
in a big under-furnished house,
you realize it has bellows
like the pipe organ
in the corner church.

There, a lithe, graying man
manipulates the console,
opening stops, depressing keys,
dancing on the elaborate petalboard
to activate large metal pipes
displayed in the chancel.

Here, your cries and screams
echo through rooms,
vibrating each tube in succession
or simultaneously,
forming complex chords,
distinct harmonics.
Grief creates a sonic
sensation of loss that,
at first, fills the empty space
like the organist
each Sunday morning,
but as the sound grows,
the house isn't filled.
Loneliness, your
loneliness, is amplified.

Then your heart stops,
blood sloshes within each
of its four tiny chambers,
temporarily trapped
until the muscle seizes

then spews again.
Tha-thump. Tha-thump.
Tha-thump. Its insistent
beat carries on, barely

audible beneath the organ's
clicks and clacks,
whines and taps,
sighs and bellows.

This is what it was like
when you left me.

ALTUN HA

You are walking among Mayan ruins.
Awakened again from incessant American
amnesia, you remember: great civilizations rise
and fall and rise again and they are not all white
and they are not all centered in Europe and they
all leave some remains. You marvel at hundreds
of steps stacked up to platforms in the sky.
Here a coliseum with perfect acoustics—Listen—
Listen—There a room with no windows where
they did surgeries—then the limestone cooling room
to manage temperature and air flow
efficiently in 300 and 400 A. D. Look
at the jungle. Its edges don't encroach as if held
by the power of the memory, though it is clear
they are mowed by local Creoles
(here half black, half British—not French
as in the States). Young men gather
with small crocodiles, snappish mouths immobilized
with rubber bands. Holding them they say,
want to touch? want to touch? and *picture?*
picture? picture? Your guide tells you
how the Mayans created girls' perfectly round faces:
two pieces of wood placed over and under
a newborn's head. The forehead and the nose
pressed flat, so too the skull bones
as they began to fuse. You are shocked
then murmur to yourself, this is how it always
is: our bodies manipulated for beauty.
Two weeks later, back home in the States,
you will take your Iranian carpet to be cleaned.
This carpet you love, made of goat hair.
The Persian man who cleans and repairs fine rugs
for rich people will tell you derisively, *It is goat wool.*
Wool, not hair. You will say, *I know.* He will say,

These women in the villages just use it
because they have nothing else. He will say,
Your rug is not of good quality or high value.
You know. All we make in life is from what
we have around us. Much is not of high value.
Still we tie small knots on goat hair,
still we press our faces flat.

THE THREE GRACES

Charm, beauty, nature, creativity, fertility.
In childhood, we three never embodied these,
but in Paris, I see us, naked, in alabaster,
holding one another with the certainty of masonry.
Knees crooked, eyes cast to the side,
each rests her body in one hip.
I fancy myself one of three,
though only I remain—
the other two lost,
not from the impermanence of stone—
eroding edges, chips, and dings—
or from the vagaries of humanity—
pillage, domination, war—
but from the volatility of family.

I want us three to endure
like these Graces—cast and passed through time,
but here, alone, I wonder, which am I?
Not Aglaea, youngest of the three,
brilliant, splendid, shining.
She could not be me.
Nor Euphrosyne, goddess of joy;
grace and beauty incarnate.
If any, I'd be Thalia, the eldest,
goddess of banquets and other festivities,
rich, abundant. Thalia, Greek Charites of good cheer.
She is me, standing in a circle singing with my sisters,
beloved by artists, sculptors, stone masons,
chiseled with beauty and elegance.

My sorors have departed—
death, familial estrangement.
I am left alone with myths to wonder,
when you look at me,

do you see the other two?
Aglaea? Euphrosyne?
When you look at me,
do you see the missing ones?
Soft, naked, on my own,

do you wonder, who?
Who has been sacrificed?
Do you, like me,
wonder how to live
absent the sororal band of three?

A TELEPHONE MESSAGE INTERRUPTS

a perfect Sunday
your father tells you
your sister is dead
a car accident
it was immediate
she didn't suffer

childhood rivalry ends
she is now perfect—
preserved in this moment
at twenty-three

she will never buy a ramshackle house
never marry someone who fights with your sister
never forget a thank you note
a birthday
Mother's day or
Father's day

now she will always be perfect
the best daughter
the favorite

but you
you will live.

II.

OPHELIA SUMMER

Some mornings violet petals cascade
from my hair as I rinse off shampoo
They fill the bathtub
It drains slowly no matter
how much I clean
I dream of delphiniums and snapdragons and gentian
I wake with the stain of day lilies' stamen on my fingertips
Ferns and salal grow between my toes under my arms
Calla lilies bloom on my breasts
Rosemary and thyme sprout from my gums
One morning I pull sage from the back of my soft palate
Shasta daises fall from my skin when I run
the three mile loop around my neighborhood
I feel their small petals form
as my skin starts to glisten
Round yellow faces pop
before they drop to the ground
Sometimes when I extend three miles to four
gerbers form on my spine
then flutter down behind
as my feet rhythmically keep time
One summer I bloom
Standing at the flower shop
eight hours a day
my legs grow peace lilies
potted and placed in a wicker basket
for delivery to funeral homes
Green leaves sprayed with magic floral lacquer
so they glisten in teared eyes
of those who survive
I learn to make ribbons
with glued, gold letters
"Beloved Friend"
"Loving Wife"

but I cannot conjure from my flesh
two dozen pink roses
to arrange as a spray on my sister's casket.

SISTERHOOD

1. FEET

Whenever I see my dead sister
she is barefoot. It was fine
this morning at the swimming pool,
but wintertime, wrapped up
in a parka and scarf, I shudder
to see her feet completely bare,
though the funeral director said
shoes and socks weren't necessary,
and it had been hard enough
to find a dress that fit.
The mortician failed to fix
her up enough to leave the lid
open, so before the closed,
public viewing, we gathered
in private to see her face,
lacerated, abraded, sort of smashed
and, thanks to the artistry of
mortuary science, caked in make-up.
My mother screamed,
grabbed her baby's body.
My other sister peered
behind the satiny drape.
She looked up, pasty.
No shoes and you should see her legs.
They look horrible— twisted, contused.
I said, *It was a car accident.*
She said, *Look, look.* I never did.

2. DRESS

When it was time that Monday afternoon
to choose a dress for her for the funeral
I wanted sweats and a T-shirt—the outfit
we'd all, eventually, remember her in.
Instead, I picked a black and white check
with a Peter Pan collar. It was too formal
but it made mother happy. Laid out,
she looked like a child. Where was
the young woman she had become?
Tall, lithe, and hip? The dancer who
favored simplicity? And the dress
was too small, so now when I see her
walking away from me,
there's a sliver of her back showing—
desiccated skin with no circulation,
yellowed like a cheap paperback novel.
The dress, cut down the center,
is held together with eight or ten
safety pins. When I call out her name,
she turns, smiles. Facing me
she wears blue sweats, a plain, white T.
No pins pressing waxy, dead skin.

3. WASHER

At twenty-two, in her rental apartment,
she owns one.
I, in my newly-bought house,
find a behemoth left behind.
Twenty years old, drab olive green,
it hulks in the corner,
outsizing anything
I've ever owned.
The previous owners knew
it could never be removed,
and who would want to?
For the first time, I clean without quarters.
Gathering laundry in large plastic baskets,
I carry them two flights down
to the dank as a ditch
Michigan basement.
When filled, it clunks and grinds,
swishes and swirls, then spills
dirty water into the drain
or drips, drips, drips until
a drizzle runs across the floor.
Then, I never asked
how she saved for her machine,
how she moved it to each new apartment.
Then, I never imagined front-loaders
in my future kitchen,
how after her death,
my parents would donate
her washer to the Salvation Army.
I never asked her,
do your clothes pile up,
do you ever forget to remove them so they sour,
where do you dry them?
In the open air?
When you put them on,
how do they smell?

4. HAIR

Hers was never like mine. It was blonde and thin
with ends that split in summertime.
As a teenager, she dyed it with Sun-In;
harsh chemicals turned her platinum.
To wrap her hair, she cut sleeves
off old, battered, white Ts;
I wove a thick, French braid
or sported barrettes, large, handmade.
Now I've cut my hair. I hear her
constant tuts and tsks. Long hair no longer
binds us. Still I dream her:
hair, thick and lush, long at the sides.
It curls and waves in ways
it never did when she was alive.

5. HANDS

Sometimes, I see her hands
at the end of my arms.
At the gym in the aerobics room mirror,
there, for a moment her long fingers,
extended, not rigid, long, graceful,
her large knuckles, holding the pose of a dancer.
Her hands pose then release,
create a flurry of movement,
the blur of a body across the floor.
Dramatic, her hands trill with rolled "r"s,
miming an operatic diva;
they flutter when she speaks,
as though inflected by a great actress.
Sometimes, I imagine my hands
on her slender frame.
I close my eyes to conjure her;
then, eyes open, I'm startled by mine:
stubby fingers, chapped skin,
small joints, bitten nails, picked cuticles.
I look away, searching for her.
Her hands draw stories
in space between us, imagine a world
beyond the mundane. Mine grip and grasp,
reach to hold and control. Hers, open.
They describe, emphasize, extend.
She should be telling this story;
she was more descriptive than I.

6. CARS

My sisters and I swap stories.
Sordid encounters with mechanics,
stock-piling engine oil.
Indignities of not-classic-just-old
motor vehicles—detectable emissions,
unmuffleable exhaust,
an array of meaningless
but once significant broken parts.
My Mercury Sable ticks miles
beyond one hundred thousand.
Broken sun visors slap passengers
with each sharp turn,
like my old Tercel,
abandoned freeway-side
when the engine gasket blew
spewing steam and smoke
at seventy miles an hour.
Its window seal,
decayed by sun,
leaked, spawning mold
beneath rotting seats.
When I had to drive
the dog to chemo,
she wouldn't ride inside,
just sat on the curb
and cried until I called a cab.

7. CHARIOTS

In Los Angeles, my living sister
drives an old Volvo,
nursed or jerry-rigged
each year to pass
the California emissions test.
The driver's door only opens
from the outside—
she cranks the window down,
reaches out to release,
then rolls it up again.
In her mind, that Volvo is gilded
and drawn by stallions.
We romanticize our cars
in spite of our sister who died.
The sun hit her eyes.
She pulled forward.
An unseen semi down an empty
morning highway crushed
her against Oregon igneous.
I imagine her wearing a seatbelt—
we're all good that way—
still, her head hit the windshield
and the enormous engine
of the '84 Mustang—
if you've never heard it,
it roars, not a horse,
but a lion, landlocked,
ready to run when the key switches on—
it was smashed on impact.

8. RETAINER

It is lost at lunchtime
in a McDonalds
on our way to Florida.
Wrapped in a white napkin,
set on a brown tray,
forgotten until fifteen minutes
down the eight-lane interstate.
Past Valdosta, from the back seat,
my sister meekly says,
I can't find my retainer.
We chorus in response,
Are you sure? Are you sure?
and rustle around looking
for what my sister knows is lost.
Back at the arches, we look
in disbelief. Twenty bags of rubbage.
We rummage through.
My mother cries
about the six hundred
dollars the retainer
will cost if we cannot find it.
She screams, *We don't have money
to throw away.* Then, pawing
through styrofoam splotched
with special sauce, single servings
of squeezed and sprayed ketchup,
hundreds of stray French fries,
I do not know in twenty years
I will make a joke graveside:
Pity, her dying so young.
If you had known,
would you have paid
to have her teeth straightened?
Then, picking through soiled paper
for my sister's corrective,

I do not know when I sweep
my own future floors,
I will pick out pennies
from dust and dog hair—
usually, but not always.

9. WIDOW

After my sister's death,
we learn that she had been married,
but they divorced six months
before her death. Her current-in-death
boyfriend, T, just T, has long, stringy hair
and no suit for the funeral.
He asks me and my best friend
if we want to get stoned.
We do, but we don't.
I never tell my parents this.
In their grief, my parents reject
the lettered simplicity of my sister's
final squeeze and embrace
the would-be, but for the divorce,
widower. This faux son-in-law
becomes a proper finish
to my sister's abridged life.

10. MYELOMAS

Ten years after my sister's death,
I learn from my father
the would-be widower is sick.
Death is certain. I make morbid jokes.
My sister, had she not died,
would be a widow, had they not divorced,
and left with young children,
had he not had a vasectomy—
a topic of much intrafamilial conversation
when my sister was alive and dating—
before we knew of the marriage
which was, of course, after her death.
After these jokes, I urge my father,
who clearly loves this man as a son,
to go, visit him. He never does.

11. CANDLE

Three days before the eleventh
anniversary of my sister's death,
my mother calls. She reports
on the death-watch (she loves to do this)
of her faux son-in-law.
On my sister's *yartzeit*, I light the candle
at sundown. The next day,
it burns well into the evening,
hours beyond the time it should expire.
I watch a late movie,
trundle off to bed at 12:30.
The candle is still burning—
thirty-two hours after I lit it.
The next morning, my mother calls;
the beloved, not quite son-in-law
died at 10:30 p.m. Pacific Time.
That is 1:30 on my coast. I am sure
as he drew his last breath
my sister's light went out.

12. SHE AND I

We were never close.
Never dyed our hair together.
No tandem manicures.
No joint shopping excursions.
We fought.
Earlier, in the back seat
of the Caprice Classic
on family vacations
and later, on the telephone.
Before she died, I told her
no one could take her seriously.
It was the way she talked.
So fast. And breathless.
Ending every declarative
with the intonation of a question.
She dismissed me, angrily.
She said, *You don't understand
my artistic personality.*
I didn't. The dancing.
The boyfriends. Alternative
music. I disliked
them all. This is the truth:
I've loved many women
more than my sister.
Had she lived, she would
have been simply
a familial correspondent—
treacly holiday sentiments,
Hallmarked birthdays.
Occasionally, I might have
called her; late on Sundays
with an obligatory update.
But now we're closer
than we've ever been. Dead,
my sister is finally present.

DEAR LARA

If you were still alive
I would French braid
purple mini-calla lilies
in your hair to celebrate
Valentine's day like
the ones I wrapped
this morning for a woman
buying flowers for a friend's
mother. Her friend was
in Iraq, and when I swiped
her card and saw her name,
I said, *My sister's name
is Lara*, as though you were
alive. She said,
*Does she have hundreds
of music boxes with
the theme from Dr. Zhivago?
Yes*, I said. You did
when you lived, and
we played "Lara's Theme"
at your funeral. Now,
more than thirteen years
later, you have never
met my wife and
will not see the thirteen
red roses I'll bring
home tonight—
one for each year
of our shared life.
Deep red for passion.
Dark, almost black,
for grief. When I give
them to her, I'll hear
the mournful measures
of Zhivago's mistress
throbbing in their buds.

OUR FAMILY WAS BROKEN BEFORE YOU DIED

Chipped, cracked, crazed, missing pieces.
A set of heirloom china without enough
place settings to feed a family of five.
Still your death added to the distress.

Another dinner plate slipped from our hands.
Shattered teacup. Mangled fork tine.
I used to cry when things broke. Goblets,
saucers, vases. Now I keep the pieces.

Place them on the kitchen table
in ways that please my eyes. What I miss
most is how you could fill the interstices.
Without you, I make my own grout:

find work, someone to love. Gather
sand and ash and silt and plaster.
Stir in water. Mix. I create mosaics.
Piece and place, salvage and shape, set and glaze.

Someday, Lara, join me. The table
is beautiful. Dinner is at eight.

III.

BLACK STOCKINGS

For Judith,
Remembering Grace Paley and Jane Cooper

You are sad about losing two
one generation ahead of you;
I read your grief on email
but don't feel it with you.
Yes, I'm sad—both poets I love—
but also relieved. This is death
in its natural order, as it should be:
women my grandmother's age die,
and women like me scramble
to buy black stockings for funerals
because we don't keep mourning
in supply. For me, it wasn't
always like this, which I can't tell you—
it would be like last night at dinner
when I was short with a friend.
She was outraged about people
protesting dead soldiers' funerals,
How can people protest a funeral?,
she asked as if this was new,
and even though she's on my side,
I was harsh, *Americans are dying*
in Iraq because we embrace the gays,
which is true at least for the protesters,
but my words were caustic;
they startled her. I didn't care;
the sudden attention
because of the soldiers,
my friend's new-found outrage;
where was the anger
when my friends died?
James, bloated even in the casket,
skin stretched over hardened flesh.

I remember his mother's shock—
two weeks earlier, she learned
her son had AIDS, was gay.
At the funeral home—the only one
in the city that would embalm "the AIDS"—
we learn of James' brother
two years earlier, also dead, AIDS, gay.
Before his final coma, James
was still working everyday in our office;
planning a benefit, attending meetings,
but wasting, wasting away,
so with him we all ate like crazy.
I gained ten pounds, and
at his funeral, walking behind suited,
white-gloved pall-bearers,
the black stockings I'd already worn
to three funerals that month
chafed my left inner thigh.

DURIO ZIBETHINUS

You smell it first. It is unlike anything
you have ever smelled. Your hosts
tell you: this is an acquired taste—
if you were in Europe, it would be bleu cheese.
You are not in Europe. You are in
Kuala Lumpur pronounced LUMP-er.
It is your first time in Asia. It is your
first time in a Muslim country. You've always
known the importance of a Palestinian homeland,
but you understand, for the first time, the urgency
of Palestine. You talk to a bookseller; you try
to get a copy of Nadia Anjuman's book, *Gule Dudi*,
which means Dark Flower. The bookseller
wants to read your palm. He wants to read
the indentations in your skull. He holds your hands
and your head and asks you, *Are you married?*
Are you married? Are you married? He suggests
he could be a good husband for you. He confirms
from the lines on the soft side of your hand that
one person is destined for you. He questions
more and more, *Are you married?* You finally
tell him that you actually do have a husband
but she is your wife, a woman; you are a lesbian.
He goes slightly crazy. He tells you, *Your body
is a temple*, which you already know. He says,
It takes 4.5 million years to get a human form,
which you did not know and you are not sure
you believe. He says, *Why do you waste
yourself, your human form, your body, your temple
on this gay mess.* For the first time, here
in Malaysia, you realize Muslims are angry.
About Palestine. The West. The war.
You despair. You know you are not
going to get your book. Your hosts give you

a white piece of fruit. It smells strong
and pungent like sweaty socks that have sat
too long. It feels like phlegm on your fingers.
You eat it. It warms your throat. It is not
like anything you have ever eaten. You bite, then
suck its flesh off the pit with your lips. It is
the king of all fruits. It is Durian. You are a Jew.

SIX CONVERSATIONS ABOUT CANCER

For Nikki

I. THINGS DONE CHANGED

I am listening to Biggie Smalls' *Ready to Die*

I've been robbin' motherfuckers
since the slave ships / with the same clip

and I know cancer
is something our mothers
and grandmothers get.

Gimme the loot
Gimme the loot

Sure, this album has been digitally remastered;
that old cassette tape was stretched to distortion.
True, I'm driving a new, blue Nissan Maxima,
a wretched four-door, family sedan,
but my beloved Toyota Tercel finally died.

Yes, I've gotten older, but listening to Biggie
I am twenty-three and we are carousing late at night and
driving down Michigan Avenue and
playing our music really loud and eating coney dogs
and rapping with the Notorious B.I.G.

You chronic smokin', Oreo cookie eatin', pickle juice drinkin',
Chicken gristle eatin', biscuit suckin', MUTHAfucka

and we are laughing so hard we are crying and
there is no cancer in your breast.

II. ONE LYMPH NODE

Both rounds of dye
and the MRI
showed nothing
no metastasis
from the tumor
in the breast tissue
to the lymph nodes
it was good
something to celebrate
then a shadow
on an X-ray
hardness in a manual
examination
small concern persists
so the doctor insists
another surgery
a small one this time
to remove one lymph node
you tell me *it is nothing*
the doctor thinks it is nothing

III. GOLD DIGGER

You have a six-year-old daughter
and breast cancer
and I am listening to hip-hop
because it is loud and honest and crass

Met her at a beauty salon
with the baby Louis Vuitton
under her underarm

and because I want our old life back,
but I can't get it back so I just
sing into your mobile vmail:

18 years / 18 years
She got one of your kids
Got you for 18 years.

You ring me back:
It ain't all that—
you and your ghetto-ass gangsta rap
not just the men are trapped.
Click.

Beep.
Another message.
You're sick and depressed
but my battery's dead
so I don't know
until the day you go back
to the doctor after his vacation
after your surgery.

I call and I call.
I croon into the headset,

Get down girl go head get down
Get down girl go head get down.

You, driving again to the doctor
for radiation therapy prep,
leave a message on my voice mail:

The one renegade lymph node?
Benign.

IV. ANGEL

Life is one big party when you're still young
But who's gonna have your back when it's all done

You write, my oncologist, my radiology oncologist,
and my surgeon are acting like The Three Stooges,

or maybe it's just my RO and the ultrasound radiologist
who can't decide between them what procedure to do.

I write, soon you will have had more doctors then lovers.
You reply, that's a nightmare, although recently

doctors have felt me up more than any lover.
I type, take action. Change that tide.

Shorty, you're my angel, you're my darling angel
Girl, you're my friend when I'm in need

V. SURVIVOR

Less than two months post-diagnosis,
you describe yourself as a cancer survivor,

I'm a survivor (What?)
I'm gonna make it (What?)

and I suppose you are. They have cut open your chest
and tested and treated and poked and prodded,

I'm not gon give up (What?)
I'm not gon stop (What?)

but you aren't getting married for another year
because you're going to lose all of your hair
and puke your guts out,
so I am surprised you use the word survive.

I will survive (What?)
Keep on survivin' (What?)

I don't yet feel
we are surviving this.

VI. YOUR SCAR

In my twenties, women's naked breasts
were everywhere for my enjoyment:
co-op bathrooms, joint house parties, my own bedroom.

I know you want it,
the thing that makes me—

I've seen your breasts a million times.
We wear the same size bra. Yours: pink,
peach, nude, black, white, and lacy.
Always lacy. Mine: white and white and white and white.
Lace makes my nipples itch.

Now the only breasts I see regularly are mine—
viewings usually confined to the shower—
and my wife's. If I get to see other boobs at all,
they are swollen and calloused;
sucked by an infant for their comfort,
their nourishment, not mine.

My milkshake brings all the boys to the yard,
and they're like / it's better than yours.

With age our breasts are contained
in functional cotton, strapped, padded and underwired,
but I miss my past—the ease of breast access.

Damn right, it's better than yours
I can teach you, / but I have to charge

I want to see your breasts. Your small scar.
The uneven shape and size.
I worry the next chance I'll have to see such a scar
will be on my chest or the chest of my wife.

AFTER THE REVOLUTION

Blessed is the match consumed in kindling flame.
—Hannah Senesh

For Glen Johnson

We meet again by chance at the airport.
You, delayed returning home
from the islands—a birthday weekend
with your partner whom I've never met
and cannot remember his name
nor how many years it has been.
My wife and I snowed in
all weekend. We chat and,
although this is odd,
I smell your breath. There,
the warm smell when you speak,
spittle when you aspirate plosives.
It reminds me of after my sister's funeral
at the outlet mall a half hour
south of Saginaw, I collapse
into your arms at Ralph Lauren,
not crying—tears had given way
to exhaustion—but needing,
desperately, comfort. You said,
Buy new sheets, good cotton ones.
Good sheets always make everything better.
Then, I remember dinner
with a prospective donor—an auto
scion. Two decades our senior,
we asked him for money
for the gay and lesbian center
and after he committed but before
coffee, he said, *Can I touch your hair?*
Initially, flustered, then, *Sure,*
and he touched tentatively
then gently ran his hand

through your hair. *I've never touched*
another man's hair. Yours is so soft,
he said. In that moment, we both saw
longing. Not love or lust but longing
for a world where one man can touch
another's hair, and this makes me
remember our old friend who didn't
make partner at the most august
of law firms—back in '92,
was it? I tell my wife, *It was*
because she was a bulldagger.
I still see her, flat shoes, black pants,
close-cropped hair. *No*, my wife says,
she isn't at all. And I don't know how
to tell her, *yes, she is; it is just you are*
more so, but it doesn't matter
because today my wife is at the pinnacle
of her career, bulldagger or not.
Glen, we made this world.
Changed what it means to be queer.
Not you and I alone
but together with thousands.
Now I look around and see
the results of our labor, and
at last I am no longer tired.
We have some difficult days
ahead but it doesn't matter
to me now. Because I've been
to the mountaintop.
Now, I dwell in the valley.
Like anybody, I would like

to live a long life. Longevity
has its place, but here at the airport,
you near fifty, ribbing me about forty,
we are both surprised
to be alive and don't even ask
about those from the past
to not review what we have lost
when there is so much
we have gained. The world has changed
since we were friends.
We meet at an airport.
Once we were the match.
Once we were the flames.

VISITING THE GRAVE

It is Friday afternoon.
We are rushing out of town,
but I want to visit
my sister's grave;
I don't know why,
just that I have plumbed
my memory for where
the cemetery is,
taken a detour into town
with no success,
so I ask my Dad who says,
I'll go with you—just follow me—
Follow me—
It is already 5:30,
and my wife grimaces,
but this is what it is
like when we travel for family—
there is no good time for grave
visitations—so we follow my father,
who has hurt his back gardening,
to Forest Lawn where my sister
is off the main road at the first left;
earlier in the day,
after we marveled at my father's roses,
heavy with flowers,
when we were sitting
by the swimming pool,
my mother said,
I should have had a fourth,
as if that would matter
this year for the first time
when my one living sister and I both
are not home for the holidays,
as if that fourth fetus might have

grown to maturity
and been there with her, celebrating,
but our sorority was three—a trifecta—
and now there are three flowers
in front of my sister's grave,
two red geraniums, one marigold,
although my sister's body isn't here—
she was burned,
then one half spread in the Pacific
and one late spring day
my father took the other half
and buried her here
near this headstone with her name;
the pain in his back is evident as he drops
to the ground and quickly begins weeding,
soon the small flower bed is clean;
he commands, *Two watering cans,*
let it shower slowly to soak the roots;
I do just that; he crawls—
wincing from the pain—
to the graves four and five spaces over—
his grandparents; he repeats it all again
talking about how he and my mother
will be buried in the spaces between
my sister and great-grandparents,
then notes wryly,
You and your sister are on your own;
this does not worry me;
while I am showering my sister's flowers,
muddy water splashes my shoes;
the small droplets dry to browned grime
before we even reach the car
where I cry as we drive away
from my dad and his hurt back,
away from his flowers,
the well-tended grave,
to the freeway which takes us home

where I will take a soft cloth,
dampened with warm water,
and wipe the stains from my shoes.

A NEW REFRIGERATOR

I didn't actually want one, but after your mother died,
you, with a big check in your pocket, became obsessed.

I measured. We shopped and shopped. You
selected and purchased. This one. It is too big—

just barely, but still—too large for the space.
I want to return it. Get a smaller model, an easier fit.

You refuse. You want this one and only this one.
You say, *We need a carpenter.* I say, *You deal with it.*

The electric behemoth sits in the center of our kitchen floor
for months. I tell our visitors that this refrigerator is

your grief—large and in the way—transformed into my headache.
Finally, I pay the housepainter an extra three hundred

to put the refrigerator in its place. When she finishes,
I admired how perfect it is. Drawing a glass of water

from its cool interior, I cry. My anger, never at you.
I want what you got: a mother to give me

something stainless, purposefully cool and icy,
something frozen for a reason.

MY FATHER'S MIMEOGRAPH

When turned on, the machine buzzed,
but warm, it hummed. In the corner
of the basement, shining stainless,
a basin for water, drum larger than
my child head, and special paper,
the master, three pages bound
at top and bottom, carefully fed by my father
into the new Selectrix, which I covet for its
femininized name, once a Selector
now, ERA imminent, Selectrix.
I envy it for a while: the time
and care my father gives it, but it liberates
the old Underwood for my purposes—
a play, a series of YA books. Also inherited,
a stack of once-used carbon papers
to mount between two fresh white sheets
and duplicate like father. Sometimes,
the carbon leaves the tips of my fingers black,
but always I yearn for the blue
of the mimeograph. I sit in the basement
corner anticipating the warm hum;
then, when my father positions the master,
ka-chunk, ka-chunk, ka-chunk.
The magical machine whirs pages
into an imperfect stack. Warmed by electricity,
the edges curl as they dry with multiple
choices for biology and chemistry—
answers I'll eventually learn and circle—
for his ecstatic appellations.
Even grown, I crave his praise.
The other day he called me about seventy
volumes of the Britannica Great Books.
He tells me, *They are bound in leather.*
If you have the shelf space, I will buy them for you.

84.

I hear the years of his promises.
The world is black & white. Good will prevail.
If I read these seventy books,
I will have all the answers I need.
I don't have the shelf space.
I open a bottle of Waterman
encre noire; I breathe in deeply, but
the liquid pigment carefully sucked
into the reservoir behind my nib
doesn't have the inky odor I seek.

IN DREAMS

Dear Lara, Do you know Greta still dreams
about you? I don't, which is fine. Your life,
your death reminded me of what is divine:

daily life. Like the pictures that litter my shelves.
Hundreds. All framed. Yet only two of you,
dear Lara. Do you know: Greta still dreams

about you. It worries me. You, dead eight years.
I listen to her dreams but want to scream, "Move on from
her death! Remind me, what is divine?

The living are divine!" If I did say that and
you, alive, heard it, you would laugh,
Lara. You know Greta. She dreams

big dreams and tries to love them into truth,
which is why, I think, she holds so tightly to
you as if rewinding death, setting back time.

Yet, we know, time only marches forward;
there will be no more pictures snapped of you.
Dear Lara, do you know Greta still dreams
your death? Remind me, again, what is divine?

PESACH 5766

Cyndi Lauper has re-released her CD acoustically.
A bunch of artists—hip-hop, rock, reggae, and soul—
cover her iconic songs. We buy it at Barnes & Noble,
listen in the car on the Saturday afternoon when cherry
blossoms are in full bloom. I drive and hold back tears
as I hear *Time After Time* again. I'm wearing the last present
my dead sister ever gave me: a white, long-sleeved jersey
from the Utah School of Massage; I have my hair pulled up
and back in just the way she used to wear it, only now
it is the only way I wear it. I feel silly about the tears.
It's been too many years. I cover them; we buy cheese
and kosher wine; I pick a fight with my wife preferring
the bravura of anger to simpering grief; stupid,
there is no one who I love more in this world and no one
who will ever love me as much as she. Consider this:
when first we met, she had large, wet spots beneath her arms—
she perspires when she's nervous—I found it endearing;
now she wears clothes fresh each day from the dry cleaners,
and I wear them a second day, to save money?—such frugality
would shock my mother—but it's true; I wear them again
when they smell of her. A month later, after the CD, after
the covered crying in the car, after I have put away my gifted shirt
in a bottom dresser drawer, we wake early. It is dark outside.
We speak in whispers about her mother, four months after
her death. We cry. I close my eyes; I imagine us moored at sea,
adrift, awash, *If you're lost you can look and you will find me*,
we are not alone; *time after time*; I imagine us eldest sons
in homes marked by lamb's blood; the angel of death
passed over our bodies; now, each year, as commanded,
we repeat these words, *we were slaves. . . .*

SHOPPING IN BANGKOK

I ask to see the aquamarine—
      my grandmother's birthstone.
No, not earrings; a pendant, perhaps?
      There were three. Each large, well-cut.
The Thai saleswoman says,
      Very beautiful, yes?
She looks at me expectantly.
      Suddenly, I am crying:
my eighty-five-year-old grandmother
      labels everything with the name
of the one who will receive it when she dies.
      The one person who should get
this pendant if I were to give
      it to my grandmother is
the granddaughter who shares her birthstone,
      aquamarine, the granddaughter—my sister—
who nearly shared her birthday
      but is now long dead,
so I tell the saleswoman,
      No. No. It is not quite right.

THE WISDOM OF SOLOMON

It seemed like a reasonable answer
to the macabre question, *How do you
want to receive the cremains?* FedEx.
Previously, remains of cremated pets
were shipped safely, sealed in plastic,
nestled in mimicked McDonald's
Big Mac containers. We set them
on the mantle. Three weeks later,
these arrive at my office—
a large bulky box. I sign while the carrier
dusts his hands on his trousers. That night,
not quite tipsy from a shot of bourbon,
my dining companion and I heft the box
to carry it to the car. Gray grit drifts
on to our hands. We open the cardboard
to see the biodegradable urn, designed
to float ashes on water, flopped inside
uncovered.

         Humans are not
entirely ash to ash, dust to dust;
our bones, our teeth do not burn easily,
that is what my father told me.
He knew more of bodies, of what
remains, from when my sister died.
Alive she always insisted, *Cremation
then into the ocean.* My father said,
Tell your children, but as if she knew
her immature ova would never reach
conception, she repeated: *Cremation . . .*
So, we knew what to do, although
my mother resisted—*a grave, a headstone.*
In grief, she insisted. So my father
split my sister in their basement

and sent one half to the Pacific and
one half to the public cemetery in Saginaw.
Although now, with my mother-in-law's ashes
spilled in corrugation, a gray cloud settling
on the floor of my office, I know my sister,
dispersed in the Pacific and buried
underground, also has settled, unintentionally,
in the basement of my parents' house.

THE WEIRD SISTERS

I dream I'm sleeping outdoors.
It is raining. My skin, soft
from bathing in fresh water.
My hair, dirty, matted. I am wet,
my bones soft and pliable
from mud and blood, but I
am happy and I dream you living,
Lara. I dream we three weyward Sisters,
hand in hand, posters of the sea and land.
We gather by fire deep in wet,
pungent woods. Cedars, thick and dense,
barely admitting light of stars
or moon lumens. We are dancing.
Naked, dirty, unafraid. Each battered
by the world, but glowing
in our now wild lives
with the power we muster among
ourselves. We chant: *Come Sisters,*
cheer we up these sprights,
and show the best of our delights.
Thrice to thine and thrice to mine,
and thrice again, to make up nine.
When I wake, I know the truth:
I sleep each night indoors.
I shower every morning.
The weyward Sisters are no more.

KUNDALINI YOGA IN CUERNAVACA

I don the black dress,
rumpled from traveling,
and thick red mules
with cork foot beds
and soft rubber soles.
I think how practical
my attire. Two small
hills to the bus stop.
I catch the Ruta 6. I've
studied the map. I know
where I am going, but
there are questions of
travel in a country where
the language sticks
on my tongue like pepper
seeds ground into salsa.
The diesel motor grinds
slowly up the hills
to the chaotic rotary.
Natives say one needs
seis huevos—the balls of God,
Zapata, and the driver
to navigate safely. We turn
and turn again, sliding
on plastic seats. I know
I am lost. Then 80,
60, 50. I press the buzzer.
42 de los Reyes is
my destination. I am
hungry for the stretch
of barnyard animals,
for poses from another
ancient land, the promise
of strength, balance, power.
I know nothing

of the Kundalini
though walking down
the hill to the next
metal door, I remember
this is the practice
of my sister sixteen
years ago. She was home
from college on summer
break, and I was living
downstate. She said
the Kundalini rose up
through her chakras
to the crown of her head.
She said the serpent
was dancing in her spine.
She said it was her most
spiritual experience
ever. The doctors called
it a brief psychotic episode.
A few years later, I
became a Jew. I enter
the compound, walk
through the garden
to the studio, take off
the black dress, stretch
in my yoga shorts.
Together, we breath,
we move, we chant,
we rest, we meditate.
We leave pesos at the altar.
I navigate old colonial
streets home. Concrete
juts up here, crumbles
down there. I cross
uneven steps of brick,
sloped driveways.
My shoes, my feet firmly
grip the ground.

PLAYING SCRABBLE WITH MY FATHER

We both pull an 'A'
from the handsewn bag.
I take a second letter
to determine who starts.
An 'R'. You pull an 'L'
earning the right to
lay down the first word,
but this Thanksgiving
eve, we pause when
I say, *Look what the letters
spell. Alar*, you declare,
having wings, knowing
I might not know
its meaning. *No*, I say,
Lara. The sister, the
daughter who died.
We both sit in silence
imagining what
might have been
until you gather the tiles,
shake the bag,
select seven new ones.
The thoughtful silence
of our game takes flight.

PECAN PIE

My sister wants advice.
Silence would starve her.
I tell her, *Edit*. She doesn't understand.
She vomits our life onto the page—
stark action, obsession, and feeling.
Her feelings: raw, unprocessed.
I tell her, *No one wants to read
our unfiltered lives. Not even I.*
I remind her, *People want to consume us
cooked, refined, warm.* I implore,
Gather ingredients. Mix. Blend. Spoon. Bake.
She brings me a raw egg, dark corn syrup,
brown sugar, pecans in their shells.
She tells me, *Eat.*

DOPPELGÄNGER

I am startled
by how much
Claire Danes looks
like you. She is
now thirty-two.
I study her
on the new TV
show wondering,
would you flip
your hair that way?
Would your laugh
reveal your teeth?
Would you have
her blend of
confidence and
vulnerability?
Most of all,
what music would
you be listening to?

I imagine scrolling
through thousands
of songs, organized
by style and mood,
on your iPod
(an appliance you
did not live to see).
You compiled
mixed tapes as a
soundtrack for
every activity.
I imagine musical
discoveries I might
find in your remastered

digital mix. My musical
tastes are pedestrian.
I take few risks.
I want to live.

NOTES

The epigraph from "Zyklon B" are the words of Lea Rosh, a member of the board of The Memorial Foundation for Murdered Jews of Europe, quoted in "Holocaust Legacy: Germans and Jews Debate Redemption" by Richard Bernstein, *The New York Times*, October 29, 2003.

The italicized lines at the end of "After the Revolution" are from Martin Luther King's speech, "I've Been to the Mountaintop," delivered April 3, 1968 in Memphis, TN. Source: http://americanradioworks.publicradio.org/features/sayitplain/mlking.html

The italicized lines in "The Weird Sisters" are from Shakespeare's *Macbeth*. Source: http://shakespeare.mit.edu/macbeth/full.html

ACKNOWLEDGMENTS

Praise to Sibling Rivalry Press—Bryan Borland and Seth Pennington.

Gratitude to my teachers—Stanley Plumly, Michael Collier, Martha Nell Smith, Minnie Bruce Pratt, and Robin Becker.

Appreciation to fellow poets and early readers—Jenny Factor, Christopher Hennessey, Matthew Hittinger, and Lawrence Schimel.

Recognition to the following publications where some of these poems first appeared, often in a different version:

> *A & U*, "Time Piece"
> *Babel Fruit*, "Altun Ha"
> *The Barefoot Muse*, "In Dreams," reprinted in *The Best of the Barefoot Muse*
> *Beltway Poetry Quarterly*, "My Name is Ethyl," "A New Refrigerator," and "She and I"
> *Calyx*, "Hamster"
> *Del Sol Review*, "Zyklon B"
> *The Drunken Boat*, "Doppleganger"
> *Feminist Studies*, "Black Stockings" (titled "For Judith") and "After the Revolution"
> *The Gay & Lesbian Review Worldwide*, "Our Family Was Broken Before You Died"
> *Junctures: The Journal for Thematic Dialogue*, "The Former Prime Minister"
> *Literary Imagination*, "Chariots"
> *Milk and Honey: A Celebration of Jewish Lesbian Poetry* (New York: A Midsummer Night's Press, 2011), "Testing Abraham."
> *MiPOesias*, "My Father's Mimeograph"
> *Pacific Review*, "Durio Zibethinus"
> *Platte Valley Review*, "Resisting Sibilance"

Room Magazine, "Playing Scrabble with My Father"
    and "Dear Lara"
Salt River Review, "Shopping in Bangkok"
Seven Kitchens Press, The chapbook, *Sisterhood*,
    published in July 2010 includes "Sisterhood,"
    "Ophelia Summer," and "Dear Lara."
Under Our Skin, "Six Conversations about Cancer"
Women's Review of Books, "Dress" and "She and I"
    (titled "My Sister and I")

Love to many friends—Agatha Beins, Gerald Maa, Carrie
Russell, and Lawrence Schimel.

ABOUT THE POET

Julie R. Enszer, PhD, is the author of *Handmade Love* (A Midsummer Night's Press, 2010) and *Sisterhood*, a chapbook (Seven Kitchens Press, 2010). She edited *Milk & Honey: A Celebration of Jewish Lesbian Poetry* (A Midsummer Night's Press, 2011), a finalist for the Lambda Literary Award in Lesbian Poetry. Enszer is also the editor and publisher of *Sinister Wisdom*, a multicultural lesbian literary and arts journal, and a regular book reviewer. You can read more of her work at

www·JULIERENSZER·com

ABOUT THE PUBLISHER

Founded in 2010, Sibling Rivalry Press is an independent publishing house based in Alexander, Arkansas. Our mission is to publish work that disturbs and enraptures. We are proud to be the home to *Assaracus*, the world's only print journal of gay male poetry. Our titles have been honored by the American Library Association through inclusion on its annual "Over the Rainbow" list of recommended LGBT reading and by *Library Journal*, who named *Assaracus* as a best new magazine of 2011. While we champion our LGBTIQ authors and artists, we are an inclusive publishing house and welcome all authors, artists, and readers regardless of sexual orientation or identity.

www·SIBLINGRIVALRYPRESS·com

CPSIA information can be obtained at www.ICGtesting.com
Printed in the USA
BVOW08s0131071113

335649BV00001B/8/P